to:

---

from:

D1272267

CHOICES

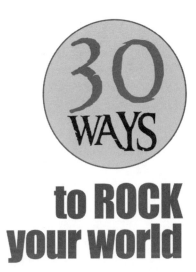

30 WAYS

to ROCK
your world

WALNUT GROVE PRESS
Nashville, TN 37202

The quoted ideas expressed in this book (but not scripture verses) are not, in all cases, exact quotations, as some have been edited for clarity and brevity. In all cases, the author has attempted to maintain the speaker's original intent. In some cases, quoted material for this book was obtained from secondary sources, primarily print media. While every effort was made to ensure the accuracy of these sources, the accuracy cannot be guaranteed. For additions, deletions, corrections or clarifications in future editions of this text, please write WALNUT GROVE PRESS.

Scripture quotations are taken from:

The Holy Bible, King James Version

The Holy Bible, New International Version (NIV) Copyright © 1973, 1978, 1984, by International Bible Society. Used by permission of Zondervan Publishing House. All rights reserved.

The New American Standard Bible®, (NASB) Copyright © 1960, 1962, 1963, 1968, 1971, 1972, 1973, 1975, 1977, 1995 by The Lockman Foundation. Used by permission.

The Holy Bible, New King James Version (NKJV) Copyright © 1982 by Thomas Nelson, Inc. Used by permission.

The Holy Bible, New Living Translation, (NLT) Copyright © 1996. Used by permission of Tyndale House Publishers, Inc., Wheaton, Illinois 60189. All rights reserved.

New Century Version®. (NCV) Copyright © 1987, 1988, 1991 by Word Publishing, a division of Thomas Nelson, Inc. All rights reserved. Used by permission.

The Message(MSG) This edition issued by contractual arrangement with NavPress, a division of The Navigators, U.S.A. Originally published by NavPress in English as THE MESSAGE: The Bible in Contemporary Language copyright 2002-2003 by Eugene Peterson. All rights reserved.

The Holman Christian Standard Bible™ (HCSB) Copyright © 1999, 2000, 2001 by Holman Bible Publishers. Used by permission.

Cover Design by Kim Russell / Wahoo Designs
Page Layout by Bart Dawson

ISBN 1-58334-258-3

Printed in the United States of America

teens

CHOICES

30 WAYS
to ROCK
your world

Table of Contents

Choices—you've already made millions of them, and you've still got millions more to make. Most of these choices are relatively small ones, like what to do at a given moment or what to say or what to wear or how to direct your thoughts. A few of your choices will be big-league decisions, like choosing to be a Christian or choosing a profession or choosing a spouse. But whatever choices you face, whether they're big, little, or somewhere in between, you can be sure of this: the quality of your choices will make a huge difference in the quality of your life.

This book contains 30 chapters that are intended to help you make choices that honor God and His only begotten Son. Each chapter contains Biblically-based, time-tested principles for finding abundance, happiness, and contentment. These principles, if taken to heart, will most certainly enrich your own life and the lives of those you love.

During the next 30 days, please try this experiment: read a chapter each day. If you're already committed to a daily time of worship, this book will enhance that experience. If you are not, the simple act of giving God a few minutes each morning will change the tone and direction of your life.

Are you facing some difficult decisions? Are you seeking to change some aspect of your life? Do you desire the eternal abundance and peace that can be yours through Christ? If so, ask for God's guidance many times each day . . . starting with a regular morning devotional. When you do, you will soon find yourself making wise choices—choices that will improve your day . . . *and* your life.

CHOICES

START BY CHOOSING GOD

The thing you should want most is God's kingdom
and doing what God wants. Then all these other
things you need will be given to you.

Matthew 6:33 NCV

You simply cannot deny this fact: your life is a series of choices. From the instant you wake up in the morning until the moment you nod off to sleep at night, you make countless decisions—decisions about the things you do, decisions about the words you speak, and decisions about the way that you choose to direct your thoughts.

Are you a believer who has been transformed by your faith in God's only begotten Son? If so, you have every reason to make smart choices. But sometimes, when the daily grind threatens to grind you up and spit you out, you may make choices that are displeasing to God. When you do, you'll pay a price because you'll forfeit the happiness and the peace that might otherwise have been yours.

So, as you pause to consider the kind of Christian you are—and the kind of Christian you want to become—ask yourself whether you're sitting on the fence or standing in the light. And then, if you sincerely want to follow in the footsteps of the One from Galilee, make choices that are pleasing to Him. He deserves no less . . . and neither, for that matter, do you.

God is voting for us all the time.
The devil is voting against us all the time.
The way we vote carries the election.

Corrie ten Boom

Good and evil both increase at compound interest.
That is why the little decisions you and I make
every day are of such infinite importance.

C. S. Lewis

Life is pretty much like a cafeteria line—
it offers us many choices, both good and bad.
The Christian must have a spiritual radar that
detects the difference not only between bad and
good but also among good, better, and best.

Dennis Swanberg

Choosing Wisely

First you make choices . . . and pretty soon those
choices begin to shape your life. That's why you must
make smart choices . . . or face the consequences
of making dumb ones.

CHOICES

I am offering you life or death, blessings or
curses. Now, choose life! . . .
To choose life is to love the Lord your God,
obey him, and stay close to him.

Deuteronomy 30:19-20 NCV

But Daniel purposed in his heart
that he would not defile himself . . . .

Daniel 1:8 KJV

Lord, help me to make choices that are pleasing
to You. Help me to be honest, patient, and kind.
And above all, help me to follow the teachings of
Jesus, not just today but every day.

Amen

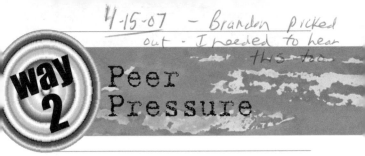

way 2

Peer Pressure

DON'T BE A PEOPLE-PLEASER . . .

Do you think I am trying to make people
accept me? No, God is the One I am trying to
please. Am I trying to please people?
If I still wanted to please people,
I would not be a servant of Christ.

Galatians 1:10 NCV

Are you a people-pleaser or a God-pleaser? Hopefully, you're far more concerned with pleasing God than you are with pleasing your friends. But even if you're a devoted Christian, you may, from time to time, feel the urge to impress your friends and acquaintances—and sometimes that urge will be *strong*.

Peer pressure can be good or bad, depending upon who your peers are and how they behave. If your friends encourage you to follow God's will and to obey His commandments, then you'll experience *positive* peer pressure, and that's a good thing. But, if your friends encourage you to do foolish things, then you're facing a different kind of peer pressure . . . and you'd better beware. When you feel pressured to do things—or to say things—that lead you away from God, you're heading straight for trouble. So don't do the "easy" thing or the "popular" thing. Do the *right* thing, and don't worry about winning any popularity contests.

Are you satisfied to follow the crowd? If so, you will probably pay a heavy price for your shortsightedness. But if you're determined to follow the One from Galilee, He will guide your steps and bless your undertakings. To sum it up, here's your choice: you can choose to please God first, or you can fall prey to peer pressure. The choice is yours—and so are the consequences.

Those who follow the crowd usually get lost in it.

Rick Warren

When we are set free from the bondage of pleasing others, when we are free from currying others' favor and others' approval—then no one will be able to make us miserable or dissatisfied. And then, if we know we have pleased God, contentment will be our consolation.

Kay Arthur

If you try to be everything to everybody, you will end up being nothing to anybody.

Vance Havner

Choosing Wisely

Face facts: Since you can't please everybody, you're better off trying to please God.

Whoever walks with the wise will become wise;
whoever walks with fools will suffer harm.

Proverbs 13:20 NLT

Blessed is the man who does not walk in
the counsel of the wicked or stand in the way
of sinners or sit in the seat of mockers.
But his delight is in the law of the LORD,
and on his law he meditates day and night.
He is like a tree planted by streams of water,
which yields its fruit in season and whose leaf
does not wither. Whatever he does prospers.

Psalm 1:1-3 NIV

Dear Lord, today I will worry less about pleasing
other people and more about pleasing You.
I will stand up for my beliefs, and I will honor You
with my thoughts, my actions, and my prayers.
And I will worship You, Father, with thanksgiving
in my heart, this day and forever.

Amen

CHOICES

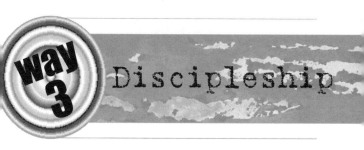

FOLLOW JESUS

Whoever serves me must follow me.
Then my servant will be with me
everywhere I am. My Father will honor
anyone who serves me.

John 12:26 NCV

With whom will you choose to walk today? Will you walk with shortsighted people who honor the ways of the world, or will you walk with the Son of God? Jesus walks with you. Are you walking with Him? Hopefully, you will choose to walk with Him today and every day of your life.

Jesus has called upon believers of every generation (and that includes you) to follow in His footsteps. And God's Word promises that when you follow in Christ's footsteps, you will learn how to live freely and lightly (Matthew 11:28-30).

Jesus doesn't want you to be a run-of-the-mill, follow-the-crowd kind of person. Jesus wants you to be a "new creation" through Him. And that's exactly what you should want for yourself, too. Nothing is more important than your wholehearted commitment to your Creator and to His only begotten Son. Your faith must never be an afterthought; it must be your ultimate priority, your ultimate possession, and your ultimate passion.

You are the recipient of Christ's love. Accept it enthusiastically and share it passionately. Jesus deserves your extreme enthusiasm; the world deserves it; and you deserve the experience of sharing it.

Jesus challenges you and me to keep
our focus daily on the cross of His will
if we want to be His disciples.

Anne Graham Lotz

A follower is never greater than his leader;
a follower never draws attention to himself.

Franklin Graham

Resolution One: I will live for God.
Resolution Two: If no one else does, I still will.

Jonathan Edwards

Choosing Wisely

If you want to be a disciple of Christ . . . follow in His footsteps, obey His commandments, talk with Him often, tell others about Him, and share His never-ending love.

Then He said to them all,
"If anyone wants to come with Me,
he must deny himself, take up his cross daily,
and follow Me."

Luke 9:23 HCSB

He has showed you, O man, what is good.
And what does the LORD require of you?
To act justly and to love mercy
and to walk humbly with your God.

Micah 6:8 NIV

Dear Lord, You sent Your Son so that I might have
abundant life and eternal life. Thank You, Father,
for my Savior, Christ Jesus. I will follow Him,
honor Him, and share His Good News,
this day and every day.
Amen

way 4 Talent

USE YOUR TALENTS

Do not neglect the spiritual gift
that is within you . . . .

1 Timothy 4:14 NASB

God knew precisely what He was doing when He gave you a unique set of talents and opportunities. And now, God wants you to use those talents for the glory of His kingdom. So here's the big question: will you choose to use those talents, or not?

Your Heavenly Father wants you to be a faithful steward of the gifts He has given you. But you live in a society that may encourage you to do otherwise. You face countless temptations to squander your time, your resources, and your talents. So you must be keenly aware of the inevitable distractions that can waste your time, your energy, and your opportunities.

Every day of your life, you have a choice to make: to nurture your talents or neglect them. When you choose wisely, God rewards your efforts, and He expands your opportunities to serve Him.

God has blessed you with unique opportunities to serve Him, and He has given you every tool that you need to do so. Today, accept this challenge: value the talent that God has given you, nourish it, make it grow, and share it with the world. After all, the best way to say "Thank You" for God's gifts is to use them.

God often reveals His direction for our lives
through the way He made us . . .
with a certain personality and unique skills.

Bill Hybels

You are the only person on earth
who can use your ability.

Zig Ziglar

In the great orchestra we call life,
you have an instrument and a song,
and you owe it to God to play them both
sublimely.

Max Lucado

Choosing Wisely

Converting talent into skill requires work:
Remember the old adage: "What we are is God's
gift to us; what we become is our gift to God."

The man who had received the five talents brought the other five. "Master," he said, "you entrusted me with five talents. See, I have gained five more." His master replied, "Well done, good and faithful servant! You have been faithful with a few things; I will put you in charge of many things. Come and share your master's happiness."

Matthew 25:20-21 NIV

Every good gift and every perfect gift is from above, and cometh down from the Father of lights.

James 1:17 KJV

Lord, You gave me talents and abilities for a reason. Let me use my talents for the glory of Your kingdom, and let me praise You always because You are the Giver of all gifts, including mine.
Amen

LEARN TO TRUST GOD

Jesus said, "Don't let your hearts be troubled.
Trust in God, and trust in me."

John 14:1 NCV

It's easy to talk about trusting God, but when it comes to actually trusting Him, that's considerably harder. Why? Because genuine trust in God requires more than words; it requires a willingness to follow God's lead and a willingness to obey His commandments (these, by the way, are not easy things to do).

Have you spent more time talking about Christ than walking in His footsteps? If so, God wants to have a little chat with you. And, if you're unwilling to talk to Him, He may take other actions in order to grab your attention.

Thankfully, whenever you're willing to talk with God, He's willing to listen. And, the instant that you decide to place Him squarely in the center of your life, He will respond to that decision with blessings that are too unexpected to predict and too numerous to count.

The next time you find your courage tested to the limit, lean upon God's promises. Trust His Son. Remember that God is always near and that He is your protector and your deliverer. When you are worried, anxious, or afraid, call upon Him. God can handle your troubles infinitely better than you can, so turn them over to Him. Remember that God rules both mountaintops and valleys—with limitless wisdom and love—now and forever.

Are you serious about wanting God's guidance to
become the person he wants you to be?
The first step is to tell God that you know you can't
manage your own life; that you need his help.

Catherine Marshall

Trusting God doesn't change our circumstances.
Perfect trust in Him changes us.

Charles Swindoll

Make the least of all that goes and the most of
all that comes. Don't regret what is past.
Cherish what you have. Look forward to
all that is to come. And most important of all,
rely moment by moment on Jesus Christ.

Gigi Graham Tchividjian

Choosing Wisely

In God we trust? You bet! One of the most
important lessons that you can ever learn is to
trust God for everything—not some things, not most
things . . . everything!

Whoever listens to what is taught will succeed,
and whoever trusts the Lord will be happy.

Proverbs 16:20 NCV

For the LORD God is our light and our protector.
He gives us grace and glory. No good thing
will the LORD withhold from those who do
what is right. O LORD Almighty,
happy are those who trust in you.

Psalm 84:11-12 NLT

Dear Lord, as I take the next steps on
my life's journey, let me take them with You.
Whatever the coming day may bring,
I will thank You for the opportunity to
live abundantly. I will be Your faithful,
faith-filled servant, Lord—and I will trust You—
this day and forever.
Amen

way 6

Self-acceptance

BE YOURSELF

... He [God] who began a good work in you
will carry it on to completion . . . .

Philippians 1:6 NIV

Are you your own worst critic? And in response to that criticism, are you constantly trying to transform yourself into a person who meets society's expectations but not God's expectations? If so, it's time to become a little more understanding of the person you see whenever you look into the mirror.

Being patient with other people can be difficult. But sometimes, we find it even more difficult to be patient with ourselves. We have high expectations and lofty goals. We want to receive God's blessings now, not later. And, of course, we want our lives to unfold according to our own wishes and our own timetables—not God's. Yet throughout the Bible, we are instructed that patience is the companion of wisdom. Proverbs 16:32 teaches us that "Patience is better than strength" (NCV). God's message, then, is clear: we must be patient with all people—including ourselves.

Millions of words have been written about various ways to improve self-image and increase self-esteem. Yet, maintaining a healthy self-image is, to a surprising extent, a matter of doing three things: (1) Obeying God (2) Thinking healthy thoughts (3) Finding a purpose for your life that pleases your Creator and yourself.

CHOICES

The Bible affirms the importance of self-acceptance by exhorting believers to love others as they love themselves (Matthew 22:37-40). Furthermore, the Bible teaches that when we genuinely open our hearts to Him, God accepts us just as we are. And, if He accepts us—faults and all—then who are we to believe otherwise?

Being loved by Him whose opinion matters most gives us the security to risk loving, too—even loving ourselves.

Gloria Gaither

You are valuable just because you exist. Not because of what you do or what you have done, but simply because you are.

Max Lucado

Choosing Wisely

Don't be too hard on yourself: you don't have to be perfect to be wonderful.

Blessed are those who do not condemn themselves.

Romans 14:22 NLT

For you made us only a little lower than God,
and you crowned us with glory and honor.

Psalm 8:5 NLT

Lord, I'm certainly not perfect, but You love me
just as I am. Thank You for Your love and
for Your Son. And, help me to become
the person that You want me to become.

Amen

CHOOSE THE RIGHT CROWD

A friend loves you all the time,
and a brother helps in time of trouble.

Proverbs 17:17 NCV

Some friendships help us honor God; these friendships should be nurtured. Other friendships place us in situations where we are tempted to dishonor God by disobeying His commandments; friendships such as these have the potential to do us great harm.

Because we tend to become like our friends, we must choose our friends carefully. Because our friends influence us in ways that are both subtle and powerful, we must ensure that our friendships are pleasing to God. When we spend our days in the presence of godly believers, we are blessed, not only by those friends but also by our Creator.

Are you hanging out with people who make you a better Christian, or are you spending time with people who encourage you to stray from your faith? The answer to this question will have a surprising impact on the condition of your spiritual health. Why? Because peer pressure is very real and very powerful. So, one of the best ways to ensure that you follow Christ is to find fellow believers who are willing to follow Him with you.

Many elements of society seek to mold you into a more worldly being; God, on the other hand, seeks to mold you into a new being, a new creation through Christ, a being that is most certainly *not* conformed to this world. If you are to please God, you must resist the pressures that society seeks to impose upon you, and you must choose, instead, to follow in the footsteps of His only begotten Son.

We long to find someone who has been where we've been, who shares our fragile skies, who sees our sunsets with the same shades of blue.

Beth Moore

Friendship is one of the sweetest joys of life. Many might have failed beneath the bitterness of their trial had they not found a friend.

C. H. Spurgeon

Choosing Wisely

Remember the first rule of friendship: it's the Golden one, and it starts like this: "Do unto others . . ." [Matthew 7:12].

As iron sharpens iron, a friend sharpens a friend.

Proverbs 27:17 NLT

Whoever walks with the wise will become wise;
whoever walks with fools will suffer harm.

Proverbs 13:20 NLT

Lord, thank You for my friends.
Let me be a trustworthy friend to others,
and let my love for You be reflected
in my genuine love for them.
Amen

DO THE RIGHT THING EVERY TIME

Do what God's teaching says;
when you only listen and do nothing,
you are fooling yourselves.

James 1:22 NCV

As Christians, we must do our best to make sure that our actions are accurate reflections of our beliefs. Our theology must be demonstrated, not only by our words but, more importantly, by our actions. In short, we should be practical believers, quick to act whenever we see an opportunity to serve God.

English clergyman Thomas Fuller observed, "He does not believe who does not live according to his beliefs." These words are most certainly true. We may proclaim our beliefs to our hearts' content, but our proclamations will mean nothing—to others or to ourselves—unless we accompany our words with deeds that match. The sermons that we live are far more compelling than the ones we preach.

Like it or not, your life is an accurate reflection of your creed. If this fact gives you cause for concern, don't bother talking about the changes that you intend to make—make them. And then, when your good deeds speak for themselves—as they most certainly will—don't interrupt.

Do noble things, do not dream them all day long.

Charles Kingsley

If doing a good act in public will excite others to do more good, then "Let your Light shine to all." Miss no opportunity to do good.

John Wesley

Let us not be content to wait and see what will happen, but give us the determination to make the right things happen.

Peter Marshall

Choosing Wisely

When it comes to telling the world about your relationship with God . . . your actions speak much more loudly than your words . . . so behave accordingly.

CHOICES

Therefore, get your minds ready for action,
being self-disciplined, and set your hope
completely on the grace to be brought to you
at the revelation of Jesus Christ. As obedient
children, do not be conformed to the desires of
your former ignorance but, as the One
who called you is holy, you also are to be
holy in all your conduct.

1 Peter 1:13-15 HCSB

Dear Lord, let my words and actions show
the world the changes that You have made
in my life. You sent Your Son so that I might have
abundant life and eternal life. Thank You, Father,
for my Savior, Christ Jesus. I will follow Him,
honor Him, and share His Good News,
this day and every day.
Amen

DATE THE RIGHT PERSON

Do not be unequally yoked together with unbelievers. For what fellowship has righteousness with lawlessness? And what communion has light with darkness?

2 Corinthians 6:14 NKJV

If you're officially "single and dating," you know from firsthand experience that dating isn't easy! And if you're like most folks, you'll probably agree that finding the right person can be, at times, an exercise in "trial and error"—with a decided emphasis on "error." So, if you've found "Mr. or Miss Right," thank the Good Lord for your good fortune. But if you're still looking, here are some things to consider:

1. Place God first in every aspect of your life, including your dating life: He deserves first place, and any relationship that doesn't put Him there is the wrong relationship for you. (Exodus 20:3)

2. Be contented where you are, even if it's not exactly where you want to end up: Think about it like this: maybe God has somebody waiting in the wings. And remember that God's timing is always best. (Philippians 4:11-12)

3. Be choosy: Don't "settle" for second-class treatment—you deserve someone who values you as a person . . . and shows it. (Psalm 40:1)

CHOICES

4. If you want to meet new people, go to the places where you are likely to bump into the kind of people you want to meet: you probably won't find the right kind of person in the wrong kind of place. (1 Corinthians 15:33)

5. Look beyond appearances: Judging other people solely by appearances is tempting, but it's foolish, shortsighted, immature, and ultimately destructive. So don't do it. (Proverbs 16:22)

Don't kid yourself: being single and dating isn't all "fun and games." Dating can be stressful, *very* stressful. And the choices that you make in the dating world can have a profound impact on every other aspect of your life. So choose carefully and prayerfully.

Choosing Wisely

Trust God: Your dating life, like every other aspect of your life, should glorify God; pray for His guidance, and follow it. (Proverbs 3:5-6)

The one who blesses others is abundantly blessed;
those who help others are helped.

Proverbs 11:25 MSG

Each of you should look not only to your own
interests, but also to the interest of others.

Philippians 2:4 NIV

Lord, I will let You rule over every aspect of my life,
including my relationships. And I know that
when I do, You will help me make choices
that are right for me, today and every day
that I live.
Amen

DECIDE HOW FAR IS TOO FAR

✳ ✳ ✳

You know the old saying, "first you eat to live,
and then you live to eat"? Well, it may be true
that the body is only a temporary thing,
but that's no excuse for stuffing your body
with food, or indulging it with sex.
Since the Master honors you with a body,
honor him with your body.

1 Corinthians 6:13 MSG

The fact that you're reading these words says something about you: you're concerned about the issue of abstinence—and you should be. You live in a society that is filled to the brim with temptations, distractions, and distortions about sex. You are bombarded with images that glamorize sex outside marriage. In fact, you are subjected to new pressures and problems that were largely unknown to earlier generations. And at every corner, or so it seems, you are confronted with the message that premarital sex is a harmless activity, something that should be considered "recreational." That message is a terrible lie with tragic consequences.

When you think about it, that decision to refuse to have sex before marriage is the only wise choice to make. First and foremost, abstinence is a part of God's plan for people who are not married. Period. But it doesn't stop there: abstinence is also the right thing to do *and* the smart thing to do.

God has a plan for your life, a plan that does not include sex before marriage. So do yourself a favor: think *very* carefully about the wisdom of waiting. Abstinence is a choice—*your* choice. Please choose wisely.

God wants you to give Him your body.
Some people do foolish things with their bodies.
God wants your body as a holy sacrifice.

Warren Wiersbe

The Bible has a word to describe "safe" sex.
It's called marriage.

Gary Smalley & John Trent

A Christian should no more defile his body
than a Jew would defile the temple.

Warren Wiersbe

Choosing Wisely

How far is too far? The Bible is right: Your body is, indeed, a temple. And if somebody wants you to trash that temple, don't do it! Furthermore, it's not okay to trash the temple "just a little bit"—don't trash it at all!

Therefore, whether you eat or drink,
or whatever you do,
do all to the glory of God.

1 Corinthians 10:31 NKJV

But I discipline my body and bring it into
subjection, lest, when I have preached to others,
I myself should become disqualified.

1 Corinthians 9:27 NKJV

Dear Lord, Your Word makes it clear
I am to honor You by honoring my body.
In every decision that I make,
I will obey my conscience
and obey Your Holy Word.
Amen

DECIDE WHAT TO WORSHIP

Honor GOD with everything you own;
give him the first and the best.
Your barns will burst,
your wine vats will brim over.

Proverbs 3:9-10 MSG

Whom will you choose to honor today? If you honor God and place Him at the center of your life, every day is a cause for celebration. But if you fail to honor your Heavenly Father, you're asking for trouble, and lots of it.

At times, your life is probably hectic, demanding, and complicated. When the demands of life leave you rushing from place to place with scarcely a moment to spare, you may fail to pause and thank your Creator for the blessings He has bestowed upon you. But that's a big mistake.

Do you sincerely seek to be a worthy servant of the One who has given you eternal love and eternal life? Then honor Him for who He is and for what He has done for you. And don't just honor Him on Sunday morning. Praise Him all day long, every day, for as long as you live . . . and then for all eternity.

The Holy Spirit testifies of Jesus.
So when you are filled with the Holy Spirit
you speak about our Lord and
really live to His honor.

Corrie ten Boom

The home should be a kind of church,
a place where God is honored.

Billy Graham

We honor God by asking for great things when
they are part of His promise. We dishonor Him and
cheat ourselves when we ask for molehills where
He has offered mountains.

Vance Havner

Choosing Wisely

The best way to worship God . . . is to worship Him
sincerely and often.

Call upon Me in the day of trouble;
I shall rescue you, and you will honor Me.

Psalm 50:15 NASB

I am always praising you;
all day long I honor you.

Psalm 71:8 NCV

I speak Your praise, O Lord. I praise You from
the depths of my heart, and I give thanks for
Your goodness, for Your mercy, and for Your Son.
Let me honor You every day of my life
through my words and my deeds.
Let me honor You, Father, with all that I am.
Amen

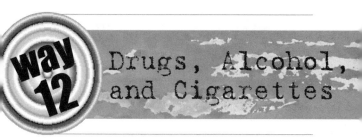

DON'T BE A DOPE

Don't be drunk with wine,
because that will ruin your life.
Instead, let the Holy Spirit fill and control you.

Ephesians 5:18 NLT

Ours is a society that glamorizes the use of drugs, alcohol, cigarettes, and other addictive substances. Why? The answer can be summed up in one word: money. Simply put, addictive substances are big money makers, so suppliers (of both legal and illegal substances) work overtime to make certain that people like you sample their products. The suppliers need a steady stream of new customers because the old ones are dying off (fast), so they engage in a no-holds-barred struggle to find new users—or more accurately, new abusers.

The dictionary defines *addiction* as "the compulsive need for a habit-forming substance; the condition of being habitually and compulsively occupied with something." That definition is accurate but incomplete. For Christians, addiction has an additional meaning: it means compulsively worshipping something other than God.

Unless you're living on a deserted island, you know people who are full-blown addicts—probably lots of people. If you, or someone you love, is suffering from the blight of addiction, remember this: Help is available. Plenty of people have experienced addiction and lived to tell about it . . . so don't give up hope.

And if you're one of those fortunate people who hasn't started experimenting with addictive substances, congratulations! You have just spared yourself a lifetime of headaches *and* heartaches.

One reason I'm a teetotaler is that
I got so disgusted being mistreated due to
a man's drinking to excess that I never have
wanted to run the risk of mistreating
my own family by drinking.

Jerry Clower

A man may not be responsible for his last drink,
but he certainly was for the first.

Billy Graham

Choosing Wisely

When it comes to the trap of addiction . . .
it's easier to stay out than it is to get out.

Watch out! Don't let me find you living
in careless ease and drunkenness,
and filled with the worries of this life.
Don't let that day catch you unaware.

Luke 21:34 NLT

It is better not to eat meat or drink wine or
do anything that will cause your brother or
sister to sin. Your beliefs about these things
should be kept secret between you and God.
People are happy if they can do what they
think is right without feeling guilty.

Romans 14:21-22 NCV

Dear Lord, you have instructed me to care for
my body, and I will obey You. I will be mindful of
the destructive power of addiction, and I will avoid
the people, the places, and the substances
that can entrap my sprit and destroy my life.

Amen

CHOOSE THE RIGHT KIND OF ATTITUDE

Fix your thoughts on what is true and honorable and right. Think about things that are pure and lovely and admirable. Think about things that are excellent and worthy of praise.

Philippians 4:8 NLT

Thoughts are intensely powerful things. Our thoughts have the power to lift us up or drag us down; they have the power to energize us or deplete us, to inspire us to greater accomplishments or to make those accomplishments impossible.

How will you choose to direct your thoughts today? Will you obey the words of Philippians 4:8 by dwelling upon those things that are honorable, true, and worthy of praise? Or will you allow your thoughts to be hijacked by the negativity that seems to dominate our troubled world.

Are you fearful, angry, bored, or worried? Are you so preoccupied with the concerns of this day that you fail to thank God for the promise of eternity? Are you confused, bitter, or pessimistic? If so, God wants to have a little talk with you.

God intends that you experience joy and abundance, but He will not force His joy upon you; you must claim it for yourself. It's up to you to celebrate the life that God has given you by focusing your mind upon "whatever is of good repute." Today, spend more time thinking about your blessings, and less time fretting about your hardships. Then, take time to thank the Giver of all things good for gifts that are, in truth, far too numerous to count.

The things we think are the things that feed
our souls. If we think on pure and lovely things,
we shall grow pure and lovely like them;
and the converse is equally true.

Hannah Whitall Smith

It is the thoughts and intents of the heart
that shape a person's life.

John Eldredge

No more imperfect thoughts.
No more sad memories. No more ignorance.
My redeemed body will have a redeemed mind.
Grant me a foretaste of that perfect mind
as you mirror your thoughts in me today.

Joni Eareckson Tada

Choosing Wisely

Good thoughts create good deeds. Good
thoughts lead to good deeds and bad thoughts lead
elsewhere. So guard your thoughts accordingly.

You were taught, with regard to
your former way of life, to put off your old self,
which is being corrupted by its deceitful desires;
to be made new in the attitude of your minds;
and to put on the new self, created to be like
God in true righteousness and holiness.

Ephesians 4:22-24 NIV

Keep your eyes focused on what is right,
and look straight ahead to what is good.

Proverbs 4:25 NCV

Lord, I pray for an attitude that is Christlike.
Whatever my situation, whether good or bad,
happy or sad, let me respond with an attitude of
optimism, faith, and love for You.
Amen

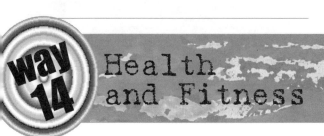
CHOOSE A HEALTHY LIFESTYLE

I discipline my body like an athlete,
training it to do what it should.
Otherwise, I fear that after preaching to others
I myself might be disqualified.

1 Corinthians 9:27 NLT

Are you shaping up or spreading out? Do you eat sensibly and exercise regularly, or do you spend most of your time on the couch with a Twinkie in one hand and a clicker in the other? Are you choosing to treat your body like a temple or a trash heap? How you answer these questions will help determine *how long* you live and *how well* you live.

Physical fitness is a choice, a choice that requires discipline—it's as simple as that. But here's the catch: understanding the need for discipline is easy, but leading a disciplined life can be hard. Why? Because it's usually more fun to eat a second piece of cake than it is to jog a second lap around the track. But, as we survey the second helpings that all too often find their way on to our plates, we should consider this: as Christians, we are instructed to lead disciplined lives, and when we behave in undisciplined ways, we are living outside God's will.

We live in a world in which leisure is glorified and consumption is commercialized. But God has other plans. He did not create us for lives of gluttony or laziness; He created us for far greater things.

God has a plan for every aspect of your life, and His plan includes provisions for your physical health. But, He expects you to do your fair share of the work! In a world that is chock-full of tasty temptations, you may find it all too easy to make unhealthy choices. Your challenge, of course, is to resist those unhealthy temptations by every means you can, including prayer. And rest assured: when you ask for God's help, He will give it.

The simple fact is that if we sow a lifestyle that is in direct disobedience to God's reveled Word, we ultimately reap disaster.

Charles Swindoll

Choosing Wisely

Taking responsibility: Simply put, it's up to you to assume the ultimate responsibility for your health. So if you're fighting the battle of the bulge (the bulging waistline, that is), don't waste your time blaming the fast food industry—or anybody else, for that matter. It's your body, and it's your responsibility to take care of it.

Whatever you eat or drink or whatever you do,
you must do all for the glory of God.

1 Corinthians 10:31 NLT

Therefore, I urge you, brothers, in view of
God's mercy, to offer your bodies as living
sacrifices, holy and pleasing to God—
this is your spiritual act of worship.

Romans 12:1 NIV

CHOICES

Heavenly Father, help me make my lifestyle
a healthy lifestyle. I need to eat right,
exercise right, and make good choices.
Guide me in those decisions that
I might honor You.
Amen

DECIDE HOW TO SPEND YOUR DAY
(and Your Life)

So teach us to number our days,
that we may gain a heart of wisdom.

Psalm 90:12 NKJV

Time is a precious, nonrenewable gift from God. But sometimes, we treat our time here on earth as if it were not a gift at all: We may be tempted to waste time in countless ways, and when we do so, we pay a high price for our misplaced priorities.

An important element of our stewardship to God is the way that we choose to spend the time He has entrusted to us. Each waking moment holds the potential to help a friend or aid a stranger, to say a kind word or think a noble thought, or offer a heartfelt prayer. Our challenge, as believers, is to use our time wisely in the service of God's work and in accordance with His plan for our lives.

How are you choosing to spend the time that God has given you? Are you investing your life wisely, or are you wasting precious days rushing after the countless distractions and temptations that the world has to offer?

As you establish priorities for your day and your life, remember that each new day is a special treasure to be savored and celebrated. As a Christian, you have much to celebrate and much to do. It's up to you, and you alone, to honor God for the gift of time by using that gift wisely.

The more time you give to something,
the more you reveal its importance
and value to you.

Rick Warren

The work of God is appointed.
There is always enough time to do the will of God.

Elisabeth Elliot

To choose time is to save time.

Francis Bacon

Choosing Wisely

If possible, establish a certain time each day when you remove yourself from all distractions; during this time, concentrate on high-priority tasks.

To every thing there is a season, and a time to every purpose under the heaven: A time to be born, and a time to die; a time to plant, and a time to pluck up that which is planted; A time to kill, and a time to heal; a time to break down, and a time to build up; A time to weep, and a time to laugh; a time to mourn, and a time to dance; A time to cast away stones, and a time to gather stones together; a time to embrace, and a time to refrain from embracing; A time to get, and a time to lose; a time to keep, and a time to cast away; A time to rend, and a time to sew; a time to keep silence, and a time to speak; A time to love, and a time to hate; a time of war, and a time of peace.

Ecclesiastes 3:1-8 KJV

Dear Lord, You have given me a wonderful gift: time here on earth. Let me use it wisely today and every day that I live.
Amen

CHOOSE TO SERVE OTHERS

The one who blesses others is abundantly blessed;
those who help others are helped.

Proverbs 11:25 MSG

The words of Jesus are clear: the greatest men and women in this world are not the big-shots who jump up on stage and hog the spotlight; the greatest among us are those who are willing to become humble servants.

Are you willing to become a servant for Christ? Are you willing to pitch in and make the world a better place, or are you determined to keep all your blessings to yourself? Hopefully, you are determined to follow Christ's example by making yourself an unselfish servant to those who need your help.

Today, you may be tempted to take more than you give. But if you feel the urge to be selfish, resist that urge with all your might. Don't be stingy, selfish, or self-absorbed. Instead, serve your friends quietly and without fanfare. Find a need and fill it . . . humbly. Lend a helping hand . . . anonymously. Share a word of kindness . . . with quiet sincerity. As you go about your daily activities, remember that the Savior of all humanity made Himself a servant, and we, as His followers, must do so too.

If the attitude of servanthood is learned,
by attending to God as Lord. Then, serving others
will develop as a very natural way of life.

Eugene Peterson

There are times when we are called to love,
expecting nothing in return. There are times when
we are called to give money to people who will
never say thanks, to forgive those who won't
forgive us, to come early and stay late
when no one else notices.

Max Lucado

I have discovered that when I please Christ,
I end up inadvertently serving others
far more effectively.

Beth Moore

Choosing Wisely

Jesus modeled servanthood. Follow His example,
even when service to others requires sacrifice on
your part.

Be devoted to one another in brotherly love.
Honor one another above yourselves.

Romans 12:10 NIV

Each of you should look not only to your own
interests, but also to the interest of others.

Philippians 2:4 NIV

Father in heaven, when Jesus humbled Himself
and became a servant, He also became
an example for His followers. Today, as I serve
my family and friends, I do so in the name of Jesus,
my Lord and Master. Guide my steps, Father,
and let my service be pleasing to You.

Amen

DECIDE HOW TO MANAGE MONEY

Keep your lives free from the love of money,
and be satisfied with what you have.

Hebrews 13:5 NCV

"So much stuff to shop for, and so little time . . ."
These words seem to describe the priorities of our
21st-century world. Hopefully, you're not building
your life around your next visit to the local mall—but
you can be sure that many people are.

Our society is in love with money and the things
that money can buy. God is not. God cares about
people, not possessions, and so must we. We must,
to the best of our abilities, love our neighbors as
ourselves, and we must, to the best of our abilities,
resist the mighty temptation to place possessions
ahead of people.

Money, in and of itself, is not evil; worshipping
money is. So today, as you prioritize matters of
importance for you and yours, remember that God
is almighty, but the dollar is not.

Are you choosing to make money your master?
If so, it's time to reorder your priorities by turning
your thoughts and your prayers to more important
matters. And, it's time to begin storing up riches that
will endure throughout eternity: the spiritual kind.

One of the dangers of having a lot of money is that you may be quite satisfied with the kinds of happiness money can give and so fail to realize your need for God. If everything seems to come simply by signing checks, you may forget that you are at every moment totally dependent on God.

C. S. Lewis

Money is a mirror that, strange as it sounds, reflects our personal weaknesses and strengths with amazing clarity.

Dave Ramsey

Have you prayed about your resources lately? Find out how God wants you to use your time and your money. No matter what it costs, forsake all that is not of God.

Kay Arthur

Choosing Wisely

It's true: Money doesn't buy happiness. The secret of a happy life has less to do with material possessions and more do with your relationships—beginning with your relationship to God.

No servant can serve two masters.
Either he will hate the one and love the other,
or he will be devoted to the one and despise
the other. You cannot serve both God and Money.

Luke 16:13 NIV

Trust in your money and down you go!
But the godly flourish like leaves in spring.

Proverbs 11:28 NLT

Dear Lord, help me to think sensibly about money.
And let me always remember that
my greatest possession has nothing to do with
my checkbook; my greatest possession is
my relationship with You through Jesus Christ.
Amen

DON'T WORRY TOO MUCH

✳ ✳ ✳

Don't fret or worry. Instead of worrying, pray.
Let petitions and praises shape your worries
into prayers, letting God know your concerns.
Before you know it, a sense of God's wholeness,
everything coming together for good, will come
and settle you down. It's wonderful what happens
when Christ displaces worry at
the center of your life.

Philippians 4:6-7 MSG

Because you have the ability to think, you also have the ability to worry. Even if you're a very faithful Christian, you may be plagued by occasional periods of discouragement and doubt. Even though you trust God's promise of salvation—even though you sincerely believe in God's love and protection— you may find yourself upset by the countless details of everyday life. Jesus understood your concerns when he spoke the reassuring words found in the 6th chapter of Matthew.

Therefore I say to you, do not worry about your life, what you will eat or what you will drink; nor about your body, what you will put on. Is not life more than food and the body more than clothing? Look at the birds of the air, for they neither sow nor reap nor gather into barns; yet your heavenly Father feeds them. Are you not of more value than they? Which of you by worrying can add one cubit to his stature? . . . Therefore do not worry about tomorrow, for tomorrow will worry about its own things. Sufficient for the day is its own trouble. vv. 25-27, 34 NKJV

Where is the best place to take your worries? Take them to God. Take your troubles to Him; take your fears to Him; take your doubts to Him; take your weaknesses to Him; take your sorrows to Him . . . and leave them all there. Seek protection from the One who offers you eternal salvation; build your spiritual house upon the Rock that cannot be moved.

Perhaps you are concerned about your future, your relationships, or your finances. Or perhaps you are simply a "worrier" by nature. If so, choose to make Matthew 6 a regular part of your daily Bible reading. This beautiful passage will remind you that God still sits in His heaven and you are His beloved child. Then, perhaps, you will worry a little less and trust God a little more, and that's as it should be because God is trustworthy…and you are protected.

Worry is a cycle of inefficient thoughts whirling around a center of fear.

Corrie ten Boom

Choosing Wisely

Worried about something you said or did? If you made a mistake yesterday, the day to fix it is today. Then, you won't have to worry about it tomorrow.

CHOICES

So don't worry, saying, "What will we eat?" or "What will we drink?" or "What will we wear?" For the Gentiles eagerly seek all these things, and your heavenly Father knows that you need them. But seek first the kingdom of God and His righteousness, and all these things will be provided for you. Therefore don't worry about tomorrow, because tomorrow will worry about itself. Each day has enough trouble of its own.

Matthew 6:31-34 HCSB

Lord, sometimes, I can't seem to help myself:
I worry. Even though I know to put my trust in You,
I still become anxious about the future.
Give me the wisdom to trust in You, Father,
and give me the courage to live a life of faith,
not a life of fear.

Amen

10-8-06 / I picked it

STAND UP AGAINST EVIL

Be self-controlled and alert.
Your enemy the devil prowls around like
a roaring lion looking for someone to devour.
Resist him, standing firm in the faith . . . .

1 Peter 5:8-9 NIV

Face facts: this world is inhabited by quite a few people who are very determined to do evil things. The devil and his human helpers are working 24/7 to cause pain and heartbreak in every corner of the globe . . . including *your* corner. So you'd better beware.

In his letter to Jewish Christians, Peter offered a stern warning: "Your adversary, the devil, prowls around like a roaring lion, seeking someone to devour" (1 Peter 5:8 NASB). What was true in New Testament times is equally true in our own. Evil is indeed abroad in the world, and Satan continues to sow the seeds of destruction far and wide.

Your job, if you choose to accept it, is to recognize evil and fight it. The moment that you decide to fight evil whenever you see it, you can no longer be a lukewarm, halfhearted Christian. And, when you are no longer a lukewarm Christian, God rejoices while the devil despairs.

When will *you* choose to get serious about fighting the evils of our world? Before you answer that question, consider this: in the battle of good versus evil, the devil never takes a day off . . . and neither should you.

Rebuke the Enemy in your own name and
he laughs; command him in the name of
Christ and he flees.

John Eldredge

Light is stronger than darkness—darkness cannot
"comprehend" or "overcome" it.

Anne Graham Lotz

We are in a continual battle with
the spiritual forces of evil, but we will triumph
when we yield to God's leading and call
on His powerful presence in prayer.

Shirley Dobson

Choosing Wisely

**Some forms of evil are woven tightly into
the fabric of society.** It's your job to make sure
that you are not woven into that fabric, too.

CHOICES

Therefore submit to God. Resist the devil and he will flee from you. Draw near to God and He will draw near to you. Cleanse your hands, you sinners; and purify your hearts, you double-minded.

James 4:7-8 NKJV

Your love must be real. Hate what is evil, and hold on to what is good.

Romans 12:9 NCV

Dear Lord, give me the wisdom to recognize
evil and the courage to fight it,
today and every day of my life.
Amen

DECIDE TO FORGIVE

Be gentle with one another, sensitive.
Forgive one another as quickly and thoroughly
as God in Christ forgave you.

Ephesians 4:32 MSG

Are you the kind of guy or girl who has a tough time forgiving and forgetting? If so, welcome to the club. Most of us find it difficult to forgive the people who have hurt us. And that's too bad because life would be much simpler if we could forgive people "once and for all" and be done with it. Yet forgiveness is seldom that easy. Usually, the decision to forgive is straightforward, but the process of forgiving is more difficult. Forgiveness is a journey that requires effort, time, perseverance, and prayer.

If there exists even one person whom you have not forgiven (and that includes yourself), obey God's commandment: forgive that person today. And remember that bitterness, anger, and regret are not part of God's plan for your life. Forgiveness is.

If you sincerely wish to forgive someone, pray for that person. And then pray for yourself by asking God to heal your heart. Don't expect forgiveness to be easy or quick, but rest assured: with God as your partner, you can forgive . . . and you will.

Forgiveness is the precondition of love.
Catherine Marshall

Are you aware of the joy-stealing effect
an unforgiving spirit is having on your life?
Charles Swindoll

Give me such love for God and men
as will blot out all hatred and bitterness.
Dietrich Bonhoeffer

Choosing Wisely

Forgive . . . and keep forgiving! Sometimes,
you may forgive someone once and then, at a later
time, become angry at the very same person again.
If so, you must forgive that person again and again
. . . until it sticks!

Stop judging others, and you will not be judged.
Stop criticizing others, or it will all come back
on you. If you forgive others,
you will be forgiven

Luke 6:37 NLT

But when you are praying, first forgive anyone
you are holding a grudge against,
so that your Father in heaven
will forgive your sins, too.

Mark 11:25 NLT

Lord, just as You have forgiven me, I am going
to forgive others. When I forgive others, I not only
obey Your commandments, but I also free myself
from bitterness and regret. Forgiveness is
Your way, Lord, and I will make it my way, too.
Amen

CONTINUE TO GROW

As newborn babies want milk,
you should want the pure and simple teaching.
By it you can grow up and be saved.

1 Peter 2:2 NCV

CHOICES

When will you be a "fully-grown" Christian? Hopefully never—or at least not until you arrive in heaven! As a believer living here on planet earth, you're never "fully grown"; you always have the potential to keep growing.

In those quiet moments when you open your heart to God, the One who made you keeps remaking you. He gives you direction, perspective, wisdom, and courage.

Would you like a time-tested formula for spiritual growth? Here it is: choose to study God's Word, choose to obey His commandments, choose to pray often, and choose to live in the center of God's will. When you do, you'll never stay stuck for long. You will, instead, be a growing Christian . . . and that's precisely the kind of Christian God wants you to be.

You are either becoming more like Christ
every day or you're becoming less like Him.
There is no neutral position in the Lord.

Stormie Omartian

Spiritual growth is the process of replacing lies
with truth.

Rick Warren

Measure your growth in grace
by your sensitiveness to sin.

Oswald Chambers

Choosing Wisely

**How do you know if you can still keep growing as a
Christian?** Check your pulse. If it's still beating, then
you can still keep growing.

Grow in grace and understanding of
our Master and Savior, Jesus Christ.
Glory to the Master, now and forever! Yes!

2 Peter 3:18 MSG

Know the love of Christ which surpasses
knowledge, that you may be filled up
to all the fullness of God.

Ephesians 3:19 NASB

Dear Lord, the Bible tells me that You are at
work in my life, continuing to help me grow and to
mature in my faith. Show me Your wisdom, Father,
and let me live according to Your Word
and Your will.
Amen

FOLLOW YOUR CONSCIENCE

So I strive always to keep my conscience clear
before God and man.

Acts 24:16 NIV

It has been said that character is what we are when nobody is watching. How true. When we do things that we know aren't right, we try to hide them from our families and friends. But even then, God is watching.

Few things in life torment us more than a guilty conscience. And, few things in life provide more contentment than the knowledge that we are obeying God's commandments. A clear conscience is one of the rewards we earn when we obey God's Word and follow His will. When we follow God's will and accept His gift of salvation, our earthly rewards are never-ceasing, and our heavenly rewards are everlasting.

Billy Graham correctly observed, "Most of us follow our conscience as we follow a wheelbarrow. We push it in front of us in the direction we want to go." If that describes you, then here's a word of warning: both you and your wheelbarrow are headed for trouble.

You can sometimes keep secrets from other people, but you can never keep secrets from God. God knows what you think and what you do. And if you want to please Him, you must start with good intentions, a pure heart, and a clear conscience.

If you sincerely wish to walk with God, follow His commandments. When you do, your character will take care of itself . . . and so will your conscience. Then, as you journey through life, you won't need to look over your shoulder to see who—besides God—is watching.

To go against one's conscience is neither safe nor right. Here I stand. I cannot do otherwise.

Martin Luther

There is no pillow so soft as a clear conscience.

French Proverb

Choosing Wisely

Should you pay close attention to that little voice inside your head? You bet! Very often, your conscience will actually tell you what God wants you to do. So listen, learn, and behave accordingly.

CHOICES

Let us come near to God with a sincere heart and
a sure faith, because we have been made free
from a guilty conscience, and our bodies
have been washed with pure water.

Hebrews 10:22 NCV

I will maintain my righteousness and
never let go of it; my conscience will not
reproach me as long as I live.

Job 27:6 NIV

Lord, You have given me a conscience that tells me
right from wrong. Let me listen to that quiet voice
so that I might do Your will and follow Your Word
today and every day.

Amen

LOOK AT THE DONUT

For God has not given us a spirit of fear,
but of power and of love and of a sound mind.

2 Timothy 1:7 NLT

On the wall of a little donut shop, the sign said:

As you travel through life, brother,
Whatever be your goal,
Keep your eye upon the donut,
And not upon the hole.

Are you a Christian who keeps your eye upon the donut, or have you acquired the bad habit of looking only at the hole? Hopefully, you spend most of your waking hours looking at the donut (and thanking God for it).

Christianity and pessimism don't mix. So do yourself a favor: choose to be a hope-filled Christian. Think optimistically about your life and your future. Trust your hopes, not your fears. Take time to celebrate God's glorious creation. And then, when you've filled your heart with hope and gladness, share your optimism with your friends. They'll be better for it, and so will you. But not necessarily in that order.

CHOICES

Make the least of all that goes and the most
of all that comes. Don't regret what is past.
Cherish what you have. Look forward to
all that is to come. And most important of all,
rely moment by moment on Jesus Christ.

Gigi Graham Tchividjian

Keep your feet on the ground, but let your heart
soar as high as it will.
Refuse to be average or to surrender to the chill of
your spiritual environment.

A. W. Tozer

Choosing Wisely

Be a realistic optimist: Your attitude toward
the future will help create your future. So think
realistically about yourself and your situation while
making a conscious effort to focus on hopes, not
fears. When you do, you'll put the self-fulfilling
prophecy to work for you.

I can do everything through him
that gives me strength.

Philippians 4:13 NIV

Make me hear joy and gladness.

Psalm 51:8 NKJV

Lord, give me faith, optimism, and hope.
Let me expect the best from You, and let me look
for the best in others. Let me trust You, Lord,
to direct my life. And, let me be Your faithful,
hopeful, optimistic servant every day that I live.

Amen

CHOOSE TO BE KIND

Be kind to each other, tenderhearted,
forgiving one another, just as God
through Christ has forgiven you.

Ephesians 4:32 NLT

Kindness is a choice. Sometimes, when we feel happy or generous, we find it easy to be kind. Other times, when we are discouraged or tired, we can scarcely summon the energy to utter a single kind word. But, God's commandment is clear: He intends that we make the conscious choice to treat others with kindness and respect, no matter our circumstances, no matter our emotions.

In the busyness and confusion of daily life, it is easy to lose focus, and it is easy to become frustrated. We are imperfect human beings struggling to manage our lives as best we can, but we often fall short. When we are distracted or disappointed, we may neglect to share a kind word or a kind deed. This oversight hurts others, but it hurts us most of all.

Today, slow yourself down and be alert for people who need your smile, your kind words, or your helping hand. Make kindness a centerpiece of your dealings with others. They will be blessed, and you will be too.

CHOICES

When you launch an act of kindness out into
the crosswinds of life,
it will blow kindness back to you.

Dennis Swanberg

The mark of a Christian is that he will walk
the second mile and turn the other cheek.
A wise man or woman gives the extra effort,
all for the glory of the Lord Jesus Christ.

John Maxwell

When you extend hospitality to others,
you're not trying to impress people,
you're trying to reflect God to them.

Max Lucado

Choosing Wisely

Kind is as kind does: In order to be a kind
person, you must do kind things. Thinking about
them isn't enough. So get busy! Your family and
friends need all the kindness they can get!

A kind man benefits himself,
but a cruel man brings trouble on himself.

Proverbs 11:17 NIV

Kind words are like honey—
sweet to the soul and healthy for the body.

Proverbs 16:24 NLT

Lord, it's easy to be kind to some people
and difficult to be kind to others. Let me be kind
to all people so that I might follow
in the footsteps of Your Son.

Amen

CHOOSE TO REJOICE

✳ ✳ ✳

Rejoice in the Lord always.
I will say it again: Rejoice!

Philippians 4:4 HCSB

Have you made the choice to rejoice? If you're a Christian, you have every reason to be joyful. After all, the ultimate battle has already been won on the cross at Calvary. And if your life has been transformed by Christ's sacrifice, then you, as a recipient of God's grace, have every reason to live joyfully. Yet sometimes, amid the inevitable hustle and bustle of life-here-on-earth, you may lose sight of your blessings as you wrestle with the challenges of everyday life.

Do you seek happiness, abundance, and contentment? If so, here are some things you should do: Love God and His Son; depend upon God for strength; try, to the best of your abilities, to follow God's will; and strive to obey His Holy Word. When you do these things, you'll discover that happiness goes hand-in-hand with righteousness. The happiest people are not those who rebel against God; the happiest people are those who love God and obey His commandments.

What does life have in store for you? A world full of possibilities (of course it's up to you to seize them), and God's promise of abundance (of course it's up to you to accept it). So, as you embark upon the next phase of your journey, remember to celebrate the life that God has given you. Your Creator has blessed you beyond measure. Honor Him with your prayers, your words, your deeds, and your joy.

Some of us seem so anxious about avoiding hell that we forget to celebrate our journey toward heaven.

Philip Yancey

If you're a thinking Christian, you will be a joyful Christian.

Marie T. Freeman

Choosing Wisely

Today is a cause for celebration: Psalm 118: 24 has clear instructions for the coming day: "This is the day which the LORD has made; let us rejoice and be glad in it." Plan your day—and your life—accordingly.

Shout for joy to the LORD, all the earth.
Worship the LORD with gladness;
come before him with joyful songs.

Psalm 100:1-2 NIV

The LORD reigns; Let the earth rejoice.

Psalm 97:1 NKJV

CHOICES

Dear Lord, You have given me so many blessings;
let me celebrate Your gifts. Make me thankful,
loving, responsible, and wise. I praise You, Father,
for the gift of Your Son and for the priceless gift of
salvation. Make me be a joyful Christian,
a worthy example to others,
and a dutiful servant to You
this day and forever.
Amen

CONTROL YOUR TEMPER

Patient people have great understanding,
but people with quick tempers
show their foolishness.

Proverbs 14:29 NCV

If you're like most people, you know a thing or two (or three) about anger. After all, everybody gets mad occasionally, and you're probably no exception.

Anger is a natural human emotion that is sometimes necessary and appropriate. Even Jesus became angry when confronted with the money-changers in the temple (Matthew 21). Righteous indignation is an appropriate response to evil, but God does not intend that anger should rule our lives. Far from it.

Temper tantrums are usually unproductive, unattractive, unforgettable, and unnecessary. Perhaps that's why Proverbs 16:32 states that, "Controlling your temper is better than capturing a city" (NCV).

If you've allowed anger to become a regular visitor at your house, you should pray for wisdom, for patience, and for a heart that is so filled with forgiveness that it contains no room for bitterness. God will help you terminate your tantrums if you ask Him—and that's a good thing because anger and peace cannot coexist in the same mind.

If you permit yourself to throw too many tantrums, you will forfeit—at least for now—the peace that might otherwise be yours through Christ. So obey God's Word by turning away from anger today and every day. You'll be glad you did, and so will your family and friends.

Anger breeds remorse in the heart,
discord in the home, bitterness in the community,
and confusion in the state.

Billy Graham

Anger is the noise of the soul;
the unseen irritant of the heart;
the relentless invader of silence.

Max Lucado

When you get hot under the collar,
make sure your heart is prayer-conditioned.

Anonymous

Choosing Wisely

No more angry outbursts! If you think you're about to explode in anger, slow down, catch your breath, and walk away if you must. It's better to walk away—and keep walking—than it is to blurt out angry words that can't be un-blurted.

A hot-tempered man stirs up dissention,
but a patient man calms a quarrel.

Proverbs 15:18 NIV

When you are angry, do not sin,
and be sure to stop being angry before
the end of the day.
Do not give the devil a way to defeat you.

Ephesians 4:26-27 NCV

Lord, I can be so impatient, and I can become
so angry. Calm me down, Lord, and give me
the maturity and the wisdom to be a patient,
forgiving Christian. Just as You have forgiven me,
Father, let me forgive others so that
I can follow the example of Your Son.
Amen

PRAY ABOUT IT

If you don't know what you're doing,
pray to the Father. He loves to help.
You'll get his help, and won't be condescended
to when you ask for it. Ask boldly, believingly,
without a second thought. People who "worry
their prayers" are like wind-whipped waves.
Don't think you're going to get anything from
the Master that way, adrift at sea,
keeping all your options open.

James 1:5-8 MSG

Okay, from the looks of things, you're an extremely busy person. And perhaps, because of your demanding schedule, you've neglected to pay sufficient attention to a particularly important part of your life: the spiritual part. If so, today is the day to change, and one way to make that change is simply to spend a little more time talking with God.

God is trying to get His message through to you. Are you listening?

Perhaps, on occasion, you may find yourself overwhelmed by the press of everyday life. Perhaps you may forget to slow yourself down long enough to talk with God. Instead of turning your thoughts and prayers to Him, you may rely upon your own resources. Instead of asking God for guidance, you may depend only upon your own limited wisdom. A far better course of action is this: simply stop what you're doing long enough to open your heart to God; then listen carefully for His directions.

In all things great and small, seek God's wisdom and His grace. He hears your prayers, and He will answer.

It is impossible to overstate the need for prayer
in the fabric of family life.

James Dobson

There is no way that Christians,
in a private capacity, can do so much to promote
the work of God and advance the kingdom of
Christ as by prayer.

Jonathan Edwards

Choosing Wisely

Prayer strengthens your relationship with God . . . So pray. Martin Luther observed, "If I should neglect prayer but a single day, I should lose a great deal of the fire of faith." Those words apply to you, too. And it's up to you to live—and to pray—accordingly.

When a believing person prays,
great things happen.

James 5:16 NCV

I want men everywhere to lift up holy hands
in prayer, without anger or disputing.

1 Timothy 2:8 NIV

Lord, make me a prayerful Christian.
In good times and in bad times,
in whatever state I find myself,
let me turn my prayers to You.
You always hear my prayers, God;
let me always pray them!
Amen

CHOOSE TO LIVE ABUNDANTLY

And God will generously provide all you need.
Then you will always have everything you need
and plenty left over to share with others.

2 Corinthians 9:8 NLT

When Jesus talks of the abundant life, is He talking about material riches or earthly fame? Hardly. The Son of God came to this world, not to give it prosperity, but to give it salvation. Thankfully for Christians, our Savior's abundance is both spiritual and eternal; it never falters—even if we do—and it never dies. We need only to open our hearts to Him, and His grace becomes ours.

God's gifts are available to all, but they are not guaranteed; those gifts must be claimed by those who choose to follow Christ. As believers, we are free to accept God's gifts, or not; that choice, and the consequences that result from it, are ours and ours alone.

Are you focused on God's Word and His will for your life? Or are you focused on the distractions and temptations of a difficult word. The answer to this question will, to a surprising extent, determine the quality and the direction of your day.

If you are a thoughtful believer, you will open yourself to the spiritual abundance that your Savior offers by following Him completely and without reservation. When you do, you will receive the love, the peace, and the joy that He has promised.

CHOICES

Do you sincerely seek the riches that our Savior offers to those who give themselves to Him? Then follow Him. When you do, you will receive the love and the abundance that He has promised. Seek first the salvation that is available through a personal, passionate relationship with Christ, and then claim the joy, the peace, and the spiritual abundance that the Shepherd offers His sheep.

If we were given all we wanted here, our hearts would settle for this world rather than the next.

Elisabeth Elliot

Jesus wants Life for us, Life with a capital L.

John Eldredge

Choosing Wisely

Don't overlook God's gifts: Every sunrise represents yet another beautifully wrapped gift from God. Unwrap it; treasure it; use it; and give thanks to the Giver.

CHOICES

If you give, you will receive.
Your gift will return to you in full measure,
pressed down, shaken together to make room for
more, and running over. Whatever measure you use
in giving—large or small—it will be used
to measure what is given back to you.

Luke 6:38 NLT

My cup runs over. Surely goodness and mercy
shall follow me all the days of my life;
and I will dwell in the house of the LORD forever.

Psalm 23:5-6 NKJV

Father, thank You for the joyful, abundant life that
is mine through Christ Jesus. Guide me according
to Your will, and help me to be a worthy servant
through all that I say and do. Give me courage,
Lord, to claim the spiritual riches that
You have promised, and lead me according to
Your plan for my life, today and always.
Amen

Sept. 2006 → James took Brandon Hiking and I asked him if he would do a devotional on the mountain Since he was missing Church. They did this one.

TRUST GOD'S PLANS

✳ ✳ James picked it & I Said, "You had Church on the mountain today" I told Brandon

"I say this because I know what I am planning for you," says the Lord. "I have good plans for you, not plans to hurt you. I will give you hope and a good future."

Jeremiah 29:11 NCV

Do you think that God has big plans for you, or do think that God wants you to be a do-nothing Christian? The answer should be obvious, but just for the record, here are the facts:

1. God has plans for your life that are far grander than you can imagine.
2. It's up to you to discover those plans and accomplish them . . . or not.

God has given you many gifts, including the gift of free will; that means that you have the ability to make choices and decisions on your own. The most important decision of your life is, of course, your commitment to accept Jesus Christ as your personal Lord and Savior. And once your eternal destiny is secured, you will undoubtedly ask yourself, "What now, Lord?" If you earnestly seek God's plan for your life, you will find it . . . in time.

Sometimes, God's plans are crystal clear, but other times, He may lead you through the wilderness before He delivers you to the Promised Land. So be patient, keep praying, and keep seeking His will for your life. When you do, you'll be amazed at the marvelous things that an all-powerful, all-knowing God can do.

CHOICES

God manages perfectly, day and night, year in and year out, the movements of the stars, the wheeling of the planets, the staggering coordination of events that goes on at the molecular level in order to hold things together. There is no doubt that He can manage the timing of my days and weeks.

Elisabeth Elliot

When God speaks to you through the Bible, through prayer, through circumstances, through the church, or in some other way, he has a purpose in mind for your life.

Henry Blackaby and Claude King

Choosing Wisely

Big, bigger, and very big plans. God has very big plans in store for your life, so trust Him and wait patiently for those plans to unfold. And remember: God's timing is best.

For God is working in you,
giving you the desire to obey him
and the power to do what pleases him.

Philippians 2:13 NLT

You have made known to me the path of life;
you will fill me with joy in your presence,
with eternal pleasures at your right hand.

Psalm 16:11 NIV

Dear Lord, You have a wonderful plan for my life.
Let me discover it, trust it, and follow it
so that I can become the person
You want me to become.
Amen

MAKE THE ULTIMATE CHOICE

For God so loved the world that he gave his only Son, so that everyone who believes in him will not perish but have eternal life.

John 3:16 NLT

He was the Son of God, but He wore a crown of thorns. He was the Savior of mankind, yet He was put to death on roughhewn cross. He offered His healing touch to an unsaved world, and yet the same hands that had healed the sick and raised the dead were pierced with nails.

Jesus Christ, the Son of God, was born into humble circumstances. He walked this earth, not as a ruler of men but as the Savior of mankind. His crucifixion, a torturous punishment that was intended to end His life and His reign, instead became the pivotal event in the history of all humanity. Christ sacrificed His life on the cross so that we might have eternal life. This gift, freely given by God's only begotten Son, is the priceless possession of everyone who accepts Him as Lord and Savior.

Why did Christ endure the humiliation and torture of the cross? He did it for you. His love is as near as your next breath, as personal as your next thought, more essential than your next heartbeat.

And what must you do in response to the Savior's gifts? You must make the "ultimate choice" by welcoming Him into your heart. And then, you must conduct yourself in a manner that demonstrates to

CHOICES

all the world that your acquaintance with the Master is not a passing fancy but that it is, instead, the cornerstone and the touchstone of your life.

God has promised us abundance, peace, and eternal life. These treasures are ours for the asking; all we must do is claim them. One of the great mysteries of life is why on earth do so many of us wait so very long to lay claim to God's gifts?

Marie T. Freeman

Teach us to set our hopes on heaven,
to hold firmly to the promise of eternal life,
so that we can withstand the struggles and
storms of this world.

Max Lucado

Choosing Wisely

What a friend you have in Jesus: Jesus loves you, and He offers you eternal life with Him in heaven. Welcome Him into your heart. Now!

Don't be troubled. You trust God,
now trust in me. There are many rooms
in my father's home, and I am going to prepare
a place for you. If this were not so,
I would tell you plainly. When everything is
ready, I will come and get you, so that you
will always be with me where I am.

John 14:1-3 NLT

These things I have written to you who believe
in the name of the Son of God,
that you may know that you have eternal life.

1 John 5:13 NKJV

Lord, You have given me the gift of eternal life
through Christ Jesus. I praise You for that
priceless gift. Because I am saved, I will share
the story of Your Son and the glory of my salvation
with a world that desperately needs Your grace.

Amen

MORE
THINGS
TO THINK
ABOUT

Choices

More Ideas about ...

The greatest choice any man makes
is to let God choose for him.

Vance Havner

Just as no one can go to hell or heaven for me,
so no one can believe for me and so no one can
open or close heaven or hell for me, and no one
can drive me either to believe or disbelieve.

Martin Luther

I do not know how the Spirit of Christ performs
it, but He brings us choices through which
we constantly change, fresh and new,
into His likeness.

Joni Eareckson Tada

We are either the masters or the victims of
our attitudes. It is a matter of personal choice.
Who we are today is the result of choices
we made yesterday. Tomorrow,
we will become what we choose today.
To change means to choose to change.

John Maxwell

Choices

Choose my instruction instead of silver, knowledge rather than choice gold, for wisdom is more precious than rubies, and nothing you desire can compare with her.
Proverbs 8:10-11 NIV

If you decide for God, living a life of God-worship, it follows that you don't fuss about what's on the table at mealtimes or whether the clothes in your closet are in fashion. There is far more to your life than the food you put in your stomach, more to your outer appearance than the clothes you hang on your body. Look at the birds, free and unfettered, not tied down to a job description, careless in the care of God. And you count far more to him than birds. Has anyone by fussing in front of the mirror ever gotten taller by so much as an inch? . . . Give your entire attention to what God is doing right now, and don't get worked up about what may or may not happen tomorrow. God will help you deal with whatever hard things come up when the time comes.
Matthew 25-27, 34 MSG

Each person should do as he has decided in his heart—not out of regret or out of necessity, for God loves a cheerful giver.
2 Corinthians 9:7 HCSB

More Ideas about . . .

Walking with God

It takes real faith to begin to live the life of heaven while still upon the earth, for this requires that we rise above the law of moral gravitation and bring to our everyday living the high wisdom of God. And since this wisdom is contrary to that of the world, conflict is bound to result. This, however, is a small price to pay for the inestimable privilege of following Christ.

A. W. Tozer

Walk in the daylight of God's will because then you will be safe; you will not stumble.

Anne Graham Lotz

To walk out of His will is to walk into nowhere.

C. S. Lewis

We are meddling with God's business when we let all manner of imaginings loose, predicting disaster, contemplating possibilities instead of following, one day at a time, God's plain and simple pathway.

Elisabeth Elliot

Walking with God

I am the light of the world. Whoever follows me
will never walk in darkness, but will have the light of life.
John 8:12 NIV

Are you tired? Worn out? Burned out on religion?
Come to me. Get away with me and you'll recover your life.
I'll show you how to take a real rest. Walk with me and work
with me...watch how I do it. Learn the unforced rhythms of
grace. I won't lay anything heavy or ill-fitting on you.
Keep company with me and you'll learn to live
freely and lightly.
Matthew 11:28-30 MSG

And what does the LORD require of you?
To act justly and to love mercy and to walk
humbly with your God.
Micah 6:8 NIV

As you therefore have received Christ Jesus the Lord,
so walk in Him, having been firmly rooted and now being
built up in Him and established in your faith, just as you were
instructed, and overflowing with gratitude.
Colossians 2:6-7 NASB

People Pleasing

Pride opens the door to every other sin,
for once we are more concerned with our
reputation than our character,
there is no end to the things we will do
just to make ourselves "look good" before others.

Warren Wiersbe

It is comfortable to know that we are responsible
to God and not to man. It is a small matter
to be judged of man's judgement.

Lottie Moon

Fashion is an enduring testimony to the fact
that we live quite consciously
before the eyes of others.

John Eldredge

Never be afraid of the world's censure;
its praise is much more to be dreaded.

C. H. Spurgeon

People Pleasing

Do not answer a fool according to his folly,
or you will be like him yourself.
Proverbs 26:4 NIV

Do not carouse with drunkards and gluttons,
for they are on their way to poverty.
Too much sleep clothes a person with rags.
Proverbs 23:20-21 NLT

Stay away from a foolish man,
for you will not find knowledge on his lips.
Proverbs 14:7 NIV

My son, if sinners entice you, do not give in to them.
Proverbs 1:10 NIV

God's Word about . . .

Money

It's sobering to contemplate how much time,
effort, sacrifice, compromise, and attention
we give to acquiring and increasing our supply of
something that is totally insignificant in eternity.

Anne Graham Lotz

There is absolutely no evidence that complexity
and materialism lead to happiness.
On the contrary, there is plenty of evidence
that simplicity and spirituality lead to joy,
a blessedness that is better than happiness.

Dennis Swanberg

We own too many things
that aren't worth owning.

Marie T. Freeman

Getting a little greedy? Pray without seizing.

Anonymous

Money

Lay not up for yourselves treasures upon earth,
where moth and rust doth corrupt, and where thieves
break through and steal: but lay up for yourselves treasures
in heaven, where neither moth nor rust doth corrupt,
and where thieves do not break through nor steal:
for where your treasure is, there will your heart be also.
Matthew 6:19-21 KJV

For what will it profit a man if he gains the whole world,
and loses his own soul?
Or what will a man give in exchange for his soul?
Mark 8:36-37 NKJV

For where your treasure is, there your heart will be also.
Luke 12:34 NKJV

Doing the Right Thing

Christianity says we were created by
a righteous God to flourish and be exhilarated in
a righteous environment. God has "wired" us
in such a way that the more righteous we are,
the more we'll actually enjoy life.

Bill Hybels

A pure theology and a loose morality
will never mix.

C. H. Spurgeon

Do nothing that you would not like to be doing
when Jesus comes. Go no place where
you would not like to be found when He returns.

Corrie ten Boom

If we have the true love of God in our hearts,
we will show it in our lives. We will not have
to go up and down the earth proclaiming it.
We will show it in everything we say or do.

D. L. Moody

Doing the Right Thing

In everything set them an example by doing what is good.
Titus 2:7 NIV

Yes, each of us will have to give a personal account to God.
Romans 14:12 NLT

Light shines on the godly, and joy on those who do right.
May all who are godly be happy in the LORD
and praise his holy name.
Psalm 97:11-12 NLT

Teach me to do Your will, for You are my God;
Your Spirit is good.
Lead me in the land of uprightness.
Psalm 143:10 NKJV

God's Word about . . .

Your Attitude

Life is 10% what happens to you
and 90% how you respond to it.

Charles Swindoll

You've heard the saying,
"Life is what you make it."
That means we have a choice.
We can choose to have a life full of frustration
and fear, but we can just as easily
choose one of joy and contentment.

Dennis Swanberg

I could go through this day oblivious to
the miracles all around me,
or I could tune in and "enjoy."

Gloria Gaither

Some people complain that God
put thorns on roses, while others praise Him
for putting roses on thorns.

Anonymous

Your Attitude

Your attitude should be the same as that of Christ Jesus:
Who, being in very nature God, did not consider equality
with God something to be grasped, but made himself nothing,
taking the very nature of a servant, being made in human
likeness. And being found in appearance as a man,
he humbled himself and became obedient to death—
even death on a cross!
Philippians 2:5-8 NIV

Therefore, since Christ suffered in his body, arm yourselves also
with the same attitude, because he who has suffered
in his body is done with sin. As a result, he does not live
the rest of his earthly life for evil human desires,
but rather for the will of God.
1 Peter 4:1-2 NIV

For the word of God is living and active.
Sharper than any double-edged sword, it penetrates even to
dividing soul and spirit, joints and marrow;
it judges the thoughts and attitudes of the heart.
Hebrews 4:12 NIV

God's Word about . . .

Your Talents

Let us use the gifts of God lest they be
extinguished by our slothfulness.

John Calvin

The Lord has abundantly blessed me
all of my life. I'm not trying to pay Him back
for all of His wonderful gifts; I just realize
that He gave them to me to give away.

Lisa Whelchel

When God crowns our merits,
he is crowning nothing other than his gifts.

St. Augustine

God is still in the process of dispensing gifts,
and He uses ordinary individuals like us to
develop those gifts in other people.

Howard Hendricks

Your Talents

We all have different gifts, each of which came because of
the grace God gave us. The person who has the gift of prophecy
should use that gift in agreement with the faith. Anyone who
has the gift of serving should serve. Anyone who has the gift
of teaching should teach. Whoever has the gift of encouraging
others should encourage. Whoever has the gift of giving to
others should give freely. Anyone who has the gift of being
a leader should try hard when he leads. Whoever has the gift
of showing mercy to others should do so with joy.

Romans 12:6-8 NCV

You did not choose Me, but I chose you and appointed you
that you should go and bear fruit, and that your fruit
should remain, that whatever you ask
the Father in My name He may give you.

John 15:16 NKJV

God has given gifts to each of you from his great variety
of spiritual gifts. Manage them well so that
God's generosity can flow through you.

1 Peter 4:10 NLT

Love

Only God can give us a selfless love for others,
as the Holy Spirit changes us from within.

Billy Graham

Carve your name on hearts, not on marble.

C. H. Spurgeon

Only joyous love redeems.

Catherine Marshall

Life is a journey,
and love is what makes that journey
worthwhile.

Anonymous

Love

If I speak the languages of men and of angels,
but do not have love, I am a sounding gong or a clanging
cymbal. If I have the gift of prophecy, and understand all
mysteries and all knowledge, and if I have all faith, so that
I can move mountains, but do not have love, I am nothing.
And if I donate all my goods to feed the poor, and if I give my
body to be burned, but do not have love, I gain nothing.
Love is patient; love is kind. Love does not envy; is not boastful;
is not conceited; does not act improperly; is not selfish; is not
provoked; does not keep a record of wrongs; finds no joy in
unrighteousness, but rejoices in the truth; bears all things,
believes all things, hopes all things, endures all things. Love
never ends. But as for prophecies, they will come to an end;
as for languages, they will cease; as for knowledge, it will come
to an end. For we know in part, and we prophesy in part.
But when the perfect comes, the partial will come to an end.
When I was a child, I spoke like a child, I thought like a child,
I reasoned like a child. When I became a man, I put aside
childish things. For now we see indistinctly, as in a mirror,
but then face to face. Now I know in part, but then I will know
fully, as I am fully known. Now these three remain:
faith, hope, and love. But the greatest of these is love.

1 Corinthians 13:1-13 HCSB

Goodness

Faith never asks whether good works are to be
done, but has done them before there is time
to ask the question, and it is always doing them.

Martin Luther

Our lives, we are told, are but fleeting at best,
Like roses they fade and decay;
Then let us do good while the present is ours,
Be useful as long as we stay.

Fanny Crosby

Here lies the tremendous mystery—
that God should be all-powerful,
yet refuse to coerce. He summons us
to cooperation. We are honored in being given
the opportunity to participate in his good deeds.
Remember how He asked for help in performing
his miracles: fill the water pots,
stretch out your hand, distribute the loaves.

Elisabeth Elliot

Goodness

See that no one pays back evil for evil,
but always try to do good to each other and to everyone else.
1 Thessalonians 5:15 NLT

The good man brings good things out of the good stored up
in him, and the evil man brings evil things
out of the evil stored up in him.
Matthew 12:35 NIV

For He has satisfied the thirsty soul,
and the hungry soul He has filled with what is good.
Psalm 107:9 NASB

Do not take revenge, my friends, but leave room for God's
wrath, for it is written: "It is mine to avenge; I will repay,"
says the Lord. On the contrary: "If your enemy is hungry,
feed him; if he is thirsty, give him something to drink.
In doing this, you will heap burning coals on his head."
Do not be overcome by evil, but overcome evil with good.
Romans 12:19-21 NIV

The Future

The future lies all before us. Shall it only be
a slight advance upon what we usually do?
Ought it not to be a bound, a leap forward
to altitudes of endeavor and
success undreamed of before?

Annie Armstrong

Never be afraid to trust an unknown future
to a known God.

Corrie ten Boom

Our yesterdays present irreparable things
to us; it is true that we have lost opportunities
which will never return, but God can transform
this destructive anxiety into a constructive
thoughtfulness for the future. Let the past sleep,
but let it sleep on the bosom of Christ.
Leave the Irreparable Past in His hands,
and step out into the Irresistible Future with Him.

Oswald Chambers

The Future

Wisdom is pleasing to you.
If you find it, you have hope for the future.
Proverbs 24:14 NCV

Know that wisdom is sweet to your soul;
if you find it, there is a future hope for you,
and your hope will not be cut off.
Proverbs 24:14 NIV

If I had the gift of prophecy, and if I knew all the mysteries
of the future and knew everything about everything,
but didn't love others, what good would I be?
And if I had the gift of faith so that I could
speak to a mountain and make it move,
without love I would be no good to anybody.
1 Corinthians 13:2 NLT

God's Word about . . .

Courage

The truth of Christ brings assurance
and so removes the former problem
of fear and uncertainty.

A. W. Tozer

Daniel looked into the face of God and
would not fear the face of a lion.

C. H. Spurgeon

Take courage. We walk in the wilderness today
and in the Promised Land tomorrow.

D. L. Moody

There comes a time when we simply
have to face the challenges in our lives
and stop backing down.

John Eldredge

Courage

All you who put your hope in the Lord be strong and brave.
Psalm 31:24 NCV

Do not be afraid or discouraged.
For the LORD your God is with you wherever you go.
Joshua 1:9 NLT

I sought the LORD, and he answered me;
he delivered me from all my fears.
Psalm 34:4 NIV

The LORD is my light and my salvation—
so why should I be afraid?
The LORD protects me from danger—
so why should I tremble?
Psalm 27:1 NLT

God's Word about . . .

Envy

Contentment comes when we develop an attitude of gratitude for the important things we do have in our lives that we tend to take for granted if we have our eyes staring longingly at our neighbor's stuff.

Dave Ramsey

How can you possess the miseries of envy when you possess in Christ the best of all portions?

C. H. Spurgeon

Discontent dries up the soul.

Elisabeth Elliot

What God asks, does, or requires of others is not my business; it is His.

Kay Arthur

God's Word about . . .

Envy

We must not become conceited,
provoking one another, envying one another.
Galatians 5:26 HCSB

But if you harbor bitter envy and selfish ambition
in your hearts, do not boast about it or deny the truth.
Such "wisdom" does not come down from heaven but is earthly,
unspiritual, of the devil. For where you have envy and
selfish ambition, there you find disorder and every evil practice.
James 3:14-17 NIV

Do not fret because of evil men or be envious of the wicked ....
Proverbs 24:19 NIV

Therefore, laying aside all malice, all deceit, hypocrisy, envy,
and all evil speaking, as newborn babes,
desire the pure milk of the word, that you may grow thereby.
1 Peter 2:1-2 NKJV

Forgiveness

If Jesus forgave those who nailed Him
to the Cross, and if God forgives you and me,
how can you withhold your forgiveness
from someone else?

Anne Graham Lotz

Doing an injury puts you below your enemy;
revenging an injury makes you even with him;
forgiving an injury sets you above him!

Anonymous

Only the truly forgiven are truly forgiving.

C. S. Lewis

We cannot be right with God
until we are right with one another.

Charles Swindoll

Forgiveness

*He who says he is in the light, and hates his brother,
is in darkness until now.*
1 John 2:9 NKJV

*Have mercy on me, O God, according to your unfailing love;
according to your great compassion blot out my transgressions.
Wash away all my iniquity and cleanse me from my sin.*
Psalm 51:1-2 NIV

*If we confess our sins to him, he is faithful and just
to forgive us and to cleanse us from every wrong.*
1 John 1:9 NLT

*He who covers his sins will not prosper,
but whoever confesses and forsakes them will have mercy.*
Proverbs 28:13 NKJV

God's Love

There is no pit so deep that God's love
is not deeper still.

Corrie ten Boom

The life of faith is a daily exploration
of the constant and countless ways in which
God's grace and love are experienced.

Eugene Peterson

To be loved by God is the highest relationship,
the highest achievement,
and the highest position of life.

Henry Blackaby and Claude King

God is a God of unconditional, unremitting love,
a love that corrects and chastens
but never ceases.

Kay Arthur

God's Love

We know how much God loves us,
and we have put our trust in him. God is love,
and all who live in love live in God, and God lives in them.
1 John 4:16 NLT

That is, in Christ, he chose us before the world was made so that
we would be his holy people—people without blame before
him. Because of his love, God had already decided to
make us his own children through Jesus Christ.
That was what he wanted and what pleased him . . . .
Ephesians 1:4-5 NCV

The LORD is kind and merciful, slow to get angry,
full of unfailing love. The LORD is good to everyone.
He showers compassion on all his creation.
Psalm 145:8-9 NLT

Many sorrows come to the wicked, but unfailing love
surrounds those who trust the LORD.
Psalm 32:10 NLT